SELECTED POEMS—VOLUME ONE

Words

TO MYSELF

MICHAEL LEONARD JEWELL

ISBN: 978-0-9829756-9-5

First School Press:
firstschoolpress@gmail.com
www.firstschoolpress.com

Proofread by Krystle Berg
Formatted by Mike Jewell
Cover Design by Jay Cookingham

Cover photo: Author's home c.1960s—Benton Township, Michigan.

Printed in the United States of America

To my sibs—
John Rice, Nancy Elizabeth, Cynthia Marie
and Daniel Burton

My brothers and sisters c. 1967 at our house on Empire Avenue (cover).

L/R: Michael Leonard holding Daniel Burton, John Rice,

Nancy Elizabeth and Cynthia Marie.

THE MACABRE

TRADITION

PEOPLE

CHILDHOOD DAYS

Childhood days are soon departed,
Grown-up schemes, now imparted,
Children's wishes are glad petitions,
That end in adult stale fruition.

Children live! Today! Today!
Tomorrow is coming! Away! Away!
Breathe, and taste, and see about you,
Let your childhood days astound you,
Soon enough, you'll leave the nest,
With only memories to give you rest.

CHILDHOOD DAYS
© 2019 by Michael Leonard Jewell

To my brother John

GENTLE PEOPLE OF THE WOOD

Acorns fall in the still of the wood,
Raindrops patter where spirits stood.
Sleepy smoke—puffs and swirls,
A playground for Indian boys and girls.
Arrow makers, chip and spark,
Hard hands peel great sheets of bark.
Careful daughters pound pemmican,
And grind their corn in stony pan.
Haughty braves make known desires,
At hazy evening council fires.

GENTLE PEOPLE OF THE WOOD
© 1992, 2019 by Michael Leonard Jewell

In honor of Chiefs Pokagon and Weesaw
of the Potawatomi Indians of Michigan

CAREWORN SAILORS

Dripping pain inspires the lot,
Aching hearts, tangle and knot,
Nets encompass, thoughts entwine,
Words deliver a hope divine.
Thinkers perish,
Like careworn sailors,
Rhyme procurers,
In calmer waters.
All destined mariners,
Chasing shadows,
Soon learn from others' cries,
That today's sunset,
Is tomorrow's sunrise.

CAREWORN SAILORS
© 1992, 2019 by Michael Leonard Jewell

In honor of my Uncle Fred Martin —
A careworn sailor of World War II

THE WISEST MAN I EVER KNEW

"the glory of children are their fathers." —*Proverbs 17:6b*

The wisest man I ever knew,
Died suddenly, years ago, a few.
He perished amidst his hopes and dreams,
Whilst trying to work his work and schemes.

At times, he deemed his life a loss,
As on his bed, he turned and tossed.
He never owned his plat of land,
His life, he thought, mere ropes of sand.

The wisest man I ever knew,
Died suddenly, years ago, a few.
He gave me books and poetry,
And cultivated my legacy.

He taught me those important things,
And gave me wisdom meant for kings.
He led me young to trust the Lord,
And pointed me where the eagles soared.

THE WISEST MAN I EVER KNEW
© 2019 by Michael Leonard Jewell

In honor of my Dad who taught me how to be a man

A DAY WITH MR. LINCOLN

The morning light sent gentle rain,
upon the dusty stone,
A carriage rattles down the lane,
and halts in haven at my home.

A tall, dark gentleman tips his hat,
and sends his trap away,
To call for him late evening,
at the end of a long, long day.

I greet him with a hearty shake,
and close and lock the door,
To spend the day at sup' and cup,
and pipefuls of country lore.

I tell him what a joy it is,
to have him in my home,
To share with him a lazy hour,
to have him all alone.

He chuckles a bit and rubs his jaw,
and sips his cup of tea,
And chats of happier, healthier days,
on why he did not choose the sea.

He tells me that he hasn't been,
as comfortable as this,
Since simple days in Illinois,
before his "wedded bliss."

5

The mantle clock—ticks and chimes,
each hour as we sit,
I think that even once or twice,
he may have dozed a bit.

The dinner bell is rung in haste,
my guest and I arise,
And through the curtain's filtered lace,
I see a Nation in his eyes.

I gave him place in honored chair,
to preside and lead in prayer,
And I remember—once or twice,
he shed a subtle tear.

He made merry at the table,
and again expressed his thanks,
For such a meal he hadn't tasted,
since the days of Nancy Hanks.

He asked for another helping,
"Just a modicum on the plate!"
I smiled at his appetite,
so unusual for him, of late.

He ended by pouring in a saucer,
his coffee out to cool,
And said he hoped the President,
had not behaved himself a fool.

I assured him—I enjoyed his spark,
'Myself, was taken away!
And I hoped the weight of his office,
had been lifted for the day.

We walked into the garden,
just beyond my simple brick,
I watched him pull a radish,
and admire the lettuce thick.

I remarked that only tender shoots,
had yet bothered to come up,
And that April was a bit too cool,
for all the other stuff.

As the sky began to overcast,
and look a bit like rain,
He told me an anecdote or two,
that seemed to ease his pain.

The mist and fog, hugged to my walls,
as if it begged to enter,
I lit the lamps and stoked the fire,
as he read a recent letter.

"It's over now, we must get on,
with forgiveness and gentle healing,"
And as he spoke, I noticed that,
the church bells all were pealing.

He talked of life in the next few years,
of raising a chicken or two,
I noticed as he spoke his heart,
the yellow flame turned blue.

He asked if he might take a nap,
before the supper hour,
His legs stretched past the davenport,
with dignity and power.

I heard him moan a dreamy sigh,
his spectacles on his chest,
I wished to know, what troubled his soul,
not wanting to stop his rest.

"Sir!" I said, "The supper's on,"
after an hour or so,
I watched the cloud lift from his eyes,
and saw the nightmare go.

We sat to supper as darkness set,
more quietly than before,
Our conversation drifted,
as a knock came at the door.

He asked me if he might return,
to rest next month in May,
To sample the fare from my garden,
if but only for the day.

He thanked me for this hour of rest,
from the battle, blood and pain,
A relief from all the memories,
of the thousands that were slain.

I held his hat in the entrance hall,
and helped him with his coat,
He shook my hand for a moment or more,
and then, he had to go.

I watched his carriage race along,
the empty, darkened street,
And thought it strange, that no soldier came,
to follow up his retreat.

I finished my cup and went to bed,
still smiling about the day,
Looking forward to our next visit,
that would most surely, come in May.

A DAY WITH MR. LINCOLN
© 1992, 2019 by Michael Leonard Jewell

*In honor of President Abraham Lincoln
who perished on April 15, 1865*

To my Aunt Shirley Wesner

NATURE

SILENCE

Silence, Silence,
in my room,
Old clock ticking,
out its doom.

Sun is setting,
Colors fading,
Dust is rising,
Smoky darkness,
intertwining.

Storm clouds looming,
overhead,
The air grows heavy,
thick like lead.

Leaves are stirring,
Lightning flashing,
Thunder rumbling,
Rain is falling,
Nature trembling.

Clear and clean,
the morning's here,
Dust is settled,
over orchard and farm.

Robins caroling,
Breezes blowing,
Grasses sparkling,
Nightmare's fleeting,
In the silence,
In my room.

SILENCE
© 1992, 2019 by Michael Leonard Jewell

THE CHIMNEY SWIFT

It's been hot all day—the sun is bearing!
The heavy air upon us wearing,
An oppressive heat, dark glass nor hat can stave.
(No wing can flutter! No leaf can wave!)

But across the lake, a shadow comes,[1]
A distant staccato of thunder drums,
That cause' the fowl and beast retreat,
On muffled wings and silent feet.

A storm advances and continues to brew,
Cicadas drone in the sweltering stew.
Cattle rouse from shade and fence,
Their "looks" incredible—countenance tense!

Cranes and bitterns in the cattails hide,
Herons, startled, to the rushes fly.
Frogs and turtles and fishes dive,
As the squall line shadow from the west arrives.

Chill from the heavens meets furnace of land,
Dust devils whistle above dust and sand,
Cold vapor cotton in gray and white,
Churns and twists like steam in the night!

The chill from above and heat below,
Shudders the branches, to-and-fro,
Then, heavy drops strike plum and pear,
And flicker the leaves like a feline ear.

We hurry inside and fasten the door,
As eaves do rattle—and shutters roar!
Then in our comfy chair, we sit,
To sip our tea and ponder a bit.

But high up above in the vapor bowers,
Among the billows and alabaster towers,
The "cigar with wings"—flaps and flitters,
And sings his song of chirps and twitters.

This feathery acrobat, turns and flutters,
In a game of tag with his sisters and brothers,
And appears to dart straight up out of sight—
Then halts for a moment, and falls out of flight.

Unlike other avian clans and tribes,
He is rather behind in color and size.
The swallow and martin in bright royal blue,
Tell the gray russet swift—"your coat will not do!"

He cannot compete with the "will" or the "widow,"[2]
Their calls heard at even' from wood and dark
shadow,
And the nighthawk so brazen, at dusk and late
camp,
A gourmet with insects at our lonely street lamp.

He avoids the palace of attic and barn,
And shuns the crag, the bridge and the cairn.
He dwells not with martin on tall wooden post,
And is humble and knows he has little to boast.

14

High up on towers of chimney and stack,
A pair place' their digs along mortar and crack.
They build their nest from the farmer's wide lot,
From a beak full of twigs, they glue in a knot.

The wife lays her clutch of eggs in a bowl,
That appear half out—and half in—the brick wall.
She nestles her chicks that will never touch ground,
And feeds them small insects where e'er they be
found.

But as soon as the heat of next summer arrives,
With storms from the west and dust devils arise.
The beasts of the fields, among rushes and trees,
Will see the dark weather and instantly flee!

But as we huddle behind our glass and door,
To watch the rain, and the wind as it roars,
The swift will fly high in the canyons and bowers,
Undaunted above in his marble-head towers.

THE CHIMNEY SWIFT
© 1995, 2019 by Michael Leonard Jewell
[1] *Lake Michigan*
[2] *Whip-poor-will and the Chuck-will's-widow*

To Mrs. Rosenberg of First School, who taught me to love the birds

STORMSCAPES

On the dock a quaking grew,
The wind, terrific gales blew,
In the lathered brine were cast,
Ships and sail with mighty mast.
Clouds one-hundred miles high,
Plunged the depths from endless sky!

Only Noah's flood, can ever stand,
To match this fury against the land,
That cause' the mountains to abase,
And squalls flee sundown in disgrace.
The hurricane—a lesser blast,
Is but a freshet by contrast.

A lighthouse, doth no sailor spy,
To gain its warmth, and lullaby,
As loss of this bright human link,
Destroys all hope beneath the ink.
Poor sailors, cut from living root,
Cast forth their souls, like ripened fruit.

Aghast—the stormy petrel's cry!
Rings deep within the funnel's eye,
Nipping waves from tip to tip,
Fast driven on by an unseen whip.

Seaweeds pitch and toss in foam,
Plucked up from deep in Neptune's loam.
Starfish torn from rock and shell,
Froth in the surf and waves pell-mell.

Churning bands of golden sand,
Divide the seashore from the land.
Starving gulls and terns do hurry,
But to vanish within the slurry.

Torrents fall on steely sheets,
Bolts of liquid hell compete.
Pleiades hastens to break and run,
Now, desiring a gentler sun.

Creatures, leagues within the deep,
Look upward as to fear and weep.
All lacking mortal light and love,
They know not that their hell's above.

In every shoal and tide pool runs,
A slimy beast from nimbus guns.
Souls pressed faint, with hopelessness,
Fall flat, as shadows, to confess—
Hours on it raged . . .

Settled storm,
Deepness wet,
All is calm,
All is set.

Silent stars peer through the strands,
Of breezy wisps and fluffy bands.
Thor's hammer—now still, from heaven's dew,
Brings rest, and then, all life renew.

STORMSCAPES
© 1992, 2019 by Michael Leonard Jewell

THE WEAVER FINCH

Poor, dusty little weaver finch,
I see you all year long,
You are so very common,
A note, your only song.

You have no claim as native,
You were not called, but sent.
You came only for a visit,
And became an immigrant.

Your ragged nest hangs from my eaves,
Your bread is pauper's fare,
Your chicks fall helpless to the ground,
And no one seems to care.

I wonder if God has made you,
To show the proud elite?
That His love and care be boundless,
The ground level at His feet.

THE WEAVER FINCH
© 1992, 2019 by Michael Leonard Jewell

To Mary and Patty Wolf—fellow birders of my youth

THE GLADES OF THE FOREST

The glades of the forest,
Show forth their wonder,
With thoughts of the deer,
That fell prey to the spirits.
The mist and the rain, the mosses so green,
All grow on the north side of God's Holy Land,
That I, as a child, cannot understand.

THE GLADES OF THE FOREST
© 2019 by Michael Leonard Jewell

To the innocence and infatuation of youth

FANTASY

THE PHANTOM SKATER OF HICKORY CREEK

The leaves are shaken by late autumn blast,
On Michigan's shore from first to last,
As the icy winds and snow, compound,
To slumber the season's stormy ground,
And only the hearty-hearted will seek—
The Phantom Skater of Hickory Creek!

It goes unnoticed—this silvery vein,
That winds and twists through its rural skein,
Deluged by storms and melting snow,
This shadowy, dismal world below,
A fitting chamber for his sleep—
The Phantom Skater of Hickory Creek!

How is it that so few have heard?
Or read in print those subtle words,
About the silent moonlit nights,
That harbor his forgotten rites,
To warn the timid and the meek—
Of the Phantom Skater of Hickory Creek!

It is difficult to understand,
Why he eschews the lake and land,
Is it that he dwells a slave?
A perpetual, superficial knave?
For during the summer he is weak—
This Phantom Skater of Hickory Creek.

21

Words To Myself

On soundless, silent winter nights,
The creek glows green with elfin light,
As skater's sparks dash off his heel,
With every spin and slice of steel.
He taps the ice with brutal beak—
The Phantom Skater of Hickory Creek.

How strange to gander his attire,
Fraught with luminous spectral fire,
His skintight knickers and leathery coat,
And yards of scarf about his throat,
To watch this fellow pitch and peak—
The Phantom Skater of Hickory Creek.

Once a man fell through the ice,
Ignoring friendship's sound advice,
That sent him crashing, through a hole,
A secluded springtime skater's stroll,
That commenced the eternal trek unique—
Of the Phantom Skater of Hickory Creek.

To find him you may deem a task,
He drags no chain across a cask,
Nor peers through window, crack and door,
On Saint Joseph's deep and muddy shore,
A playground fitting to the bleak—
The Phantom Skater of Hickory Creek.

Of graveyard, he's no citizen,
He haunts no house or demon's den,
If only one could find his bones,
And put at rest his restless groans,
To forever seal this infernal freak—
The Phantom Skater of Hickory Creek.

So, if winter's face should find you coy,
A warmer clime you might enjoy,
To shun this fellow's low estate,
Of shrieking soul and streaking skate,
To forever flee the pallid cheek—
Of the Phantom Skater of Hickory Creek.

THE PHANTOM SKATER OF HICKORY CREEK
© 1992, 2019 by Michael Leonard Jewell

Dedicated to the old Berrien County legend

A WARRIOR'S DESIRE

Oh, how I desire to go down with the ship,
To glide beneath the waves of glass,
To sleep with them that went before,
To hear the bell once more.

Oh, how I desire to do battle again,
To take my place among their bones,
To pass on through that precious gate,
To join them there alone.

Oh, how I desire to make it right,
To stand again in the ranks of light,
To grasp my sword and charge once more,
To meet them all through the angel's door.

A WARRIOR'S DESIRE
© 2019 by Michael Leonard Jewell

To my brother Dan

SIR ATHELFREY
THE STOUT-HEART

Across an open field, trudging,
Belanterned, and the moonlight watching,
As western skies fast fade away,
A hooded stranger named Athelfrey,
With quarterstaff and bag in hand,
'Comes trudging, trudging across the land.

As twilight catches in the trees,
He reaches the forest on his knees,
And kisses an oaken crucifix,
While crossing head, and heart, and chest,
And shivers once or twice in thought,
To consider what his path hath wrought.

Through the tangled thorn and vine,
And shaggy branch' of twisted pine,
With vengeance hot upon his heart,
And in his bag a wooden dart,
He seeks the wicked altar beyond,
To cleanse the sacrifice thereon.

The forest is bright with dismal light,
And blinking owls and shrieking kite.
Glowworms crawl and undulate,
To mark his path and keep it straight.
Fireflies swarming—flit and dance,
As Athelfrey stumbles in a trance.

His weary frame's brought in submission,
Lest he forget his lofty mission,
As weariness overcomes his brow,
Climbing over branch and bough.
All he wants to do is rest,
In some secluded mossy nest.

His hap upon a clearing came,
So bright with lunar light and beam,
Where grass and emerald moss abound,
And warmth from rotting leaves and ground,
Lure him into gentle slumber,
To rest his bones, his soul unencumbered.

For hours he lay as one that's dead,
Upon his providential bed,
Renewing strength 'twas lost in fear,
That threatened his noble conscience sear.
Then startles he as his fever breaks,
His hunger ravenous as he wakes.

He rubs his eyes and looks about,
For what he sees is mixed with doubt,
Glowing coals and baking bread,
A skin of wine beside his head,
A mutton joint and brace of fowl,
A bowl of water and folded towel.

He shouts to find his benefactor,
Through the mocking, eerie laughter,
Of toiling creatures from beneath,
That watch and worry, while he eats.

Now his fill has rid his hunger,
Then falls he into silent slumber,
As hours more he rests his head,
On burlap pillow and mossy bed.

Then morn arise' and open eyes,
Reveal the vapor curtain skies,
Sheets and veil of gray and brown,
Bring chill and damp upon the ground.

Athelfrey resumes his journey,
Renewed in strength and vengeful fury,
Wondering who his friend might be,
That delivers bread and mystery.

Above the trees, he sees the mountain,
Where flows the scarlet, bloody fountain,
Freeing souls from tortured frames,
And lifeless forms from unknown names.

He breaks the forest quite unseen,
His wits honed sharp, senses keen,
His pathway veiled by blowing fog,
That threatens to pen his epilogue.

He enters in silence through forest gate,
And slays the sentries that hesitate,
Fitting his bloody sword in sheath,
He treads upon their broken teeth.

Stepping fast along the path,
He's guided on by holy wrath,
To slay the evil beast ahead,
That seized M'lady from off her bed.

With the path before him, in array,
Athelfrey beholds the castle gray,
Must find the beast before the dusk,
And slay him with my sword and tusk!

Athelfrey swims 'cross castle's moat,
With leather bag and sodden coat,
He gropes and feels along the wall,
To find his way to the evil hall.

Fear begins to grip and seek,
His arms and legs grow cold and weak,
His eyes and thoughts begin to mist,
As weariness makes his body list.

Beneath the murky slime he slips,
As foam and blood spew from his lips.
Death has gripped him in its maw,
Poised to crush him in its jaws.

Then on a mossy stone, he lay,
His lantern lit with cheerful ray,
His clothes now dry—he sees no friend,
Save roasting fowl in an oven therein.

Again, he feasts, to save his flesh,
Thankful to slip the Devil's mesh,
And marvels, sleeping by a pool,
That his fire burns without its fuel.

Awakened by a constant dripping,
From up above, the rocks are bleeding,
Now is his pathway marked in blood,
As his steps take hold in the scarlet mud.

He climbs the rocky stair in haste,
Hating to alter his unbroken pace,
This way unknown for years, he thinks.
Perhaps the beast knows it not, he winks.

High above the precipice,
As rocks plunge into nothingness,
He reaches to an ancient door,
That leads him to the castle's core.

He enters into a dreary hall,
That never saw a cheerful ball,
Nor graced a lady's gleeful dance,
With artful knights in sweet romance.

Words To Myself

The sun is set in amber red,
For day and night are poised to wed.
Athelfrey wonders what wicked yeast,
Will cause the rising of the beast.

He peers through broken glass and lead,
Into the courtyard stained with red,
And starts, in shock, at what he sees,
Along the stones and through the trees.

Rows of stakes surround the yard,
With tarnished knights all standing guard,
Their wicked master, enthroned beyond,
His victims all impaled thereon.

This evil prince born from below,
His wicked seed is scattered so,
He plucks the petal, still in bud,
To dip his bread in human blood.

Athelfrey in rage draws forth his sword,
And bursts upon the evil lord,
To dash away his heinous cup,
His bowl and bread of evil sup.

Foul beast! pray bid thy servants near!
For now, thy breast shall know to fear!
Treason! cries he, *Hast thou me found?*
Then utters he no more earthly sound!

Athelfrey pulls from the evil brisket,
His dripping sword all honed and whetted,
And gazes on, with moonlight shone,
The severed head and shards of bone.

He poises in ready combat stance,
To await the tarnished knight's advance.
His sword held high, to swing and slice,
His mercy, now, as cold as ice!

Then to the stones the knights do fall,
With sparks and clatter throughout the hall,
We bow to our king! they shout, as one.
To the Stout-heart! they cry, in unison.

To thee, Sir Athelfrey, we do attend!
Who freed us all from the serpent's end!
God sent thee guide through wicked wood,
To save us through thy noble good!

Then from the door comes castle's guard,
Across the bloody, shameful yard,
And in their midst in flowing dress,
Comes Athelfrey's love from dungeon's rest.

The beast—deigned through his wicked eyes,
To keep M'lady for his prize,
Now doth she weep to quell her pain,
To embrace her prince with soulful rain.

Close upon her champion's vest,
Her tears run warm down cheek and breast,
She gazes upon the bloody head,
That mocks her still—though now is dead.

Dear one, 'twas I, who sought thy good,
And cared for thee in wicked wood.
My prayers prevailed and thou wert saved,
Though I was helpless, and enslaved.

Then leaving beloved's warm embrace,
To vent her holy rage in haste,
She steps her foot in hurried pace,
To grind her heel 'pon the grinning face!

Then Athelfrey turns himself about,
To hear the people, cheer and shout!
He forgives them, leads them to atone,
They bid him reign upon the throne.

If thou wilt serve me as thy king,
And bid me wear a sovereign's ring,
Then cause to peal the churches' bells,
And burn these implements of Hell!

Then did the land enjoy a rest,
From evil fowl in evil nest,
And all proclaimed a holy day,
To honor and love Prince Athelfrey.

SIR ATHELFREY THE STOUT-HEART
© 2019 by Michael Leonard Jewell

TENDERNESS AND FAITH

STILL

Still, so still,
No blade or leaf in motion.
Soft, so softly on,
The warm air feels the ocean.

On, still on I go,
Stars and moon are sparkling.
The night is long,
The haze is gone,
But soon we'll ride together.

Happy, soon happy will come,
I cannot find you but you know where I am,
To meet me there soon—to take me away,
Where it's still,
So still,
So still.

STILL
© 1992, 2019 by Michael Leonard Jewell

To Peeps

A LONG DAY'S JOURNEY

A long day's journey,
I have known,
Of simple wood,
Of gentle stone,
Of gravel roads,
And being alone—
No Kathy in those days.

A long day's journey,
I did roam.
On endless walks,
On endless loam,
A sweetheart's kiss,
And being alone—
No Kathy in those days.

A long day's journey,
I did my best,
Writing poems,
And seeking rest,
Keeping sorrow,
In sorrow's nest—
No Kathy in those days.

A LONG DAY'S JOURNEY
© 1992, 2019 by Michael Leonard Jewell

A CERTAIN MERCY

There is a certain Mercy,
As rare as Christmas Day,
She often goes unnoticed,
She seldom comes to stay.

Mercy has two sisters,
Named Happy and Content,
The three may come to visit,
But not linger, or consent.

You may beg them stay for supper,
To have a dram more tea,
The more you seek their friendship, though—
The more they'll disagree.

You cannot win them, pleading,
They must seek you out, instead,
Their favors rarely given,
Their virtues more than bread.

You may enter at their garden's gate,
And through their windows peep,
But only gain their kindness,
If—'tis for others—that you weep.

So if you seek Content and Happy,
They'll flee before your face,
Taking sister Mercy with them—
Along with cousin Grace.

A CERTAIN MERCY
© 2019 by Michael Leonard Jewell

WAS IT NOT SWEET?

Was it not sweet?
Was it not pure?
Our first gentle kiss,
Our first tenderness.

Was it not fine?
Your garment white,
Your fragrance bright,
The bloom of your skin.

Was it not fair?
The day we sat,
The time we knew,
When our hearts were met.
Was it not sweet?

WAS IT NOT SWEET?
© 2019 by Michael Leonard Jewell

LIFE NOW EVERLASTING

Lost and lonely, out of the fold,
The wind blows through the trees so cold,
The enemy lurks in the darkness, bold,
Forcing me to my knees.

I stare into the misty glen,
No comfort can I find within,
Tears from fear, guilt from sin,
My fate I ever pine.

Now, Jesus' light shines 'pon my heart,
His mercy and grace to take my part,
His free gift cause' my sin depart,
My life now everlasting!

LIFE NOW EVERLASTING
© 2019 by Michael Leonard Jewell

In honor of Dr. Robert Vickroy

THE EMMAUS ROAD AGAIN

Let me walk the Emmaus Road,
Along with Thee—hand in hand,
Let us take our journey home,
Across the burning sand.

Teach me the Truths of Thy coming grace,
From Eden's bliss to Bethlehem's star,
Forgive my slowness to believe,
My blind eyes holden to perceive.

Turn in, turn in and stay a while,
Let not Thy footsteps pass me by,
Forever cause my heart to burn,
And vanish not from my needy side.

And while I yet on earth must dwell,
Until my change doth surely come,
Let me always at moment's whim,
Walk the Emmaus Road again.

THE EMMAUS ROAD AGAIN
© 2012, 2019 by Michael Leonard Jewell

To my wife Rita

IN THE SHADOWS

HOW DRY THE WELL

How dry the well,
No fountain here,
Young love's gone,
The same old tears.

Grayness comes,
Then the clouds,
Responsibility,
Forever loud.

Young hope's gone,
New fears here,
Tears are endless,
Death is near.

HOW DRY THE WELL
© 2019 by Michael Leonard Jewell

I WONDER

I wonder what it's like?
To hold my dreams up in my hand,
Those elusive wisps of vapor that
I cannot understand.

Those words of consolation,
That I dwell on by the hour,
Those things that others have to hold
for me do only sour.

So in conclusion, let me say,
Relief will never come,
The only feelings that I feel
are feeling rather numb.

So 'til I find a worthy path,
To free me from this pain,
I'll dwell between the sunshine and the rain.

I WONDER
© 2019 by Michael Leonard Jewell

HALF AN HOUR

From now to the time of ending,
Half an hour I would beg,
Before the final unwinding,
Before the final dreg.

Knowing no more wandering,
I'd imagine it my way,
That a half an hour might last,
From morning to the end of my day.

I'd see you through a warm spring rain,
And know your tenderness under a blue sky,
All secrets kept will be then revealed,
All truths no more a lie.

The moonlight through a fragile lace,
A final cup of tea,
Will be the outlet of my care,
The testament that is me.

HALF AN HOUR
© 2019 by Michael Leonard Jewell

IT HAD TO BE

It had to be—I died today,
My wretchedness killed me; carried me away.
A blanket of snow; it covered me,
A fathom of water, in the sea,
The setting sun; the twilight hides me,
A cubit of earth, now I will be free,
Since you left—I died today,
Pity me not—it had to be.

IT HAD TO BE
© 2019 by Michael Leonard Jewell

I DON'T TRUST

I don't trust those surly fellows,
They'll steal me surely blind,
In hopes that they'll secure me,
Is lost in futile rhyme,
In hopes that they'll ignore me,
(They creep in all around!)
The ones that plead their friendship, most,
Oft makes the slightest sound.

I DON'T TRUST
© 2019 by Michael Leonard Jewell

To times wasted amongst "friends"

THE MIGHTY PIPER

Set in a shocking century,
A life for most of me,
For I—destined four-quarters long,
Could only manage three.

I thought I'd hang around a while,
Like Burns, Berlin, and Hope,
But after only seventy-five,
I found I couldn't cope.

It takes me twice as long to shave,
To shower, and to dress,
I'm rarely up for breakfast, lunch . . .
Well, you understand the rest.

So, now I lay me down to sleep,
Perhaps 'twill be today,
There'll be no more waiting,
For the Mighty Piper to pay.

THE MIGHTY PIPER
© 2019 by Michael Leonard Jewell

With all respect and reverence to the Mighty Piper

THE MACABRE

OH, GRIM NECROPOLIS!

Oh, grim necropolis! Brightness lacking,
Gray and mossy in the shadowy wood,
Hidden, forgotten, untouched by sunlight,
Citizens within do go unsought.
Vile hasp and rusty lock—oh!
That keeps imprisoned the silent knock.

OH, GRIM NECROPOLIS!
© 2019 by Michael Leonard Jewell

WHAT HAPPENS WHEN YOU RUN AT NIGHT?

You cut your feet on thorns and briars,
Sink and slip in muck that mires,
Sting and welt your face with brambles,
Bark your legs on gravestones hidden,
Run in terror past all that hungers,
Slashed by creature' claws a-flailing,
Worried by crushing jaws a-gaping,
Ivory teeth like castanets snapping!

Then in dread you make escape,
And crawl to where you deem it safe,
Alas to thrash where leeches caress,
In the mighty bog named—*Bottomless!*

WHAT HAPPENS WHEN YOU RUN AT NIGHT?
© 2019 by Michael Leonard Jewell

To the soldiers of the Vietnam War

OH, FETID VESSEL!

Oh, fetid vessel! Made of wicker,
Fouled and stained with coffin liquor,
Dripping thick like candle fat,
Upon the marble stone thereat,
Congealed pools of distilled death,
That cannot be washed away.

OH, FETID VESSEL!
© 2019 by Michael Leonard Jewell

BLEAK OCTOBER 31ST

Harvest is done and duties met,
With lathered teams and dusty sweat.
A time of rest, and celebration,
Unfettered by toil and consternation.

Children laughing, play and run,
Unmindful of the setting sun,
Shuffling through leaves—thick and set,
A yearly carpet's surrogate.

Chilling currents of gentle wind,
Soon mingle with the warm again.
A blazing sun in horizon's pocket,
Descends into its ancient socket.

Brilliant stars—wink and shine,
Through icy clouds and creeping vine.
Moonlight shimmering—soaks the wood,
Flooding fields where harvest stood.

Breezes cease to move and toss,
Still and chill engenders frost.
Deadbolt, chain and locking pin,
Ensures that all are safe within.

৩

Much beyond the eastern section,
Where the corn hill change' direction,
Hard by, the churning swamp beyond,
Lies the murky slough and pond.

Through the scum peers glowing eyes,
Catfish gape, and croak their sighs,
Serpents wriggle—turtles snap!
Leeches suck their bloody sap.

Near a twenty-acre lake,
That turns from blue to black opaque,
Breaks a twig, and to the sky,
A thousand bats do burst on high!

Clouds of jet against the moon,
Cause' faith to falter, hearts to swoon.
Rodent eyes and dripping fang,
Comprises this unholy gang!

Far across the stubble field,
Where oak and sugar maple' yield,
Flares a point of amber light,
That smokes and dances in the night.

A closer observation sees,
A gentle clearing through the trees,
A seething cauldron in the woods,
A troika bound in leather hoods.

Now, spouting chants and speaking trouble,
Making toads and lizards bubble,
Heating their vat with sulfur flame,
Grinning—they play their wicked game!

Corn shocks stand in staggered rows,
Jack o' lantern candle's glow,
Gourds and squashes, piled in heaps,
Dreadful shadows—ghouls and creeps.

❧

An ancient house on Dismal Hill,
Seems to generate, at will,
Evil weather—rain and storm,
A fitting place for flies to swarm.

Deep beneath in dripping grotto,
Spiders hunt and dine in shadow,
Mildew, moss and mold abound,
Adorning this unhallowed ground.

Dark within a room of stone,
Comes forth a creature's awful groan.
From a wooden box arise',
Icy flesh with maggot eyes.

Creaking hinge' and rusty nails,
Squeaking rats and swishing tails,
Warty toads and salamanders,
Eat their fill of "many leggers."[1]

Behind the barn in a bramble thicket,
Walks a specter on silent picket.
Hanging from a crooked branch,
A guilty corpse in eternal trance.

A rotting cadaver lies supine,
A place for birds of prey to dine,
A rusty axe in bloody red,
Beguiles the grin of its severed head.

❧

The night's soon ending in the vale,
A shallow morning upon its trail,
All frightful signs that did astound,
Flee and vanish without a sound.

The witches and their accoutrements,
Now fade away with power spent.
Evil house where vultures soar,
Is nothing more than rock and tor.

Skulls and heads with bloody knife,
Are pumpkins, squashes, sticks in light.
Swinging corpse with eyes of coal,
Is naught but scarecrow on his pole.

So when, next "fall of leaves," is o'er,
And hay is made from grass and clover,
When specters choose to rise and walk,
And loathsome creatures choose to stalk.

Words To Myself

Secure your doors and windows tight,
And pull the curtains to bar the night,
Say your prayers upon your bed,
And pull the covers over head.

જી

Now the rising of the sun,
Cause' the evil visions, run!
Glorious Light removes the curse,
Of bleak October Thirty-first.

So is November here to cleanse,
A portent of cheerfulness, my friends,
A royal time, for thanks to be given,
To found dear memories for the children.

BLEAK OCTOBER 31st
© 2019 by Michael Leonard Jewell
[1] *Centipedes*

There is nothing in the dark that isn't there when the lights are on —
Rod Serling

TRADITION

FIRST CHRISTMAS ON THE FARM

I 'rose up early in time to dress,
So careful not to 'waken Bess,
No time for coffee, tea or bread,
'must hasten as the east glows red.

My path begins through frosted door,
To survey the stars that hover o'er,
So cold that e'en the dog stays in,
To circle his rug 'fore the fire within.

Trekking past the forest and fields,
The slowly growing dawn reveals,
A wood of fragrant evergreen,
All frosted, glowing like a dream.

As I approach with noisy feet,
On crusted snow and fallen sleet,
A flock of roosting mourning doves,
Burst skyward, as I drop my gloves.

I hurry, as my hands grow numb,
To scrutinize each bough by thumb,
To 'waken the Yuletide bush, from slumber,
With dripping sap against its lumber.

Words To Myself

I cut and saw through bark and ice,
And fell the tree with jagged slice,
To drag it 'cross the crusted snow,
With frosted beard and throbbing toe.

Shining sun so bright and cold,
As I arrive at humble home,
And through the cabin's narrow door,
I sprinkle needles on the floor.

Sweet Bess awaits me with a kiss,
While fireplace coals and coffee hiss,
Flecks of snow melt on the floor,
As I am scolded, but loved once more.

The growing heat in cheery room,
The kitchen smells and Christmas tune,
Compel the stiffened leaves and branches,
To blossom out while morn advances.

Bess is so much like a child,
With eyes aglow and manners mild,
She decorates our perfect tree,
With popcorn garland while drinking tea.

The mantle clock chimes up midday,
As bright clouds turn to ashen gray,
The blue sky fades as storm draws near,
The sunshine's but a golden smear.

Across the field, behind our house,
No pawing deer or drumming grouse,
Nor hints of life in this weary land,
Of barren tundra and lunar sand.

Then as the mantle clock strikes two,
It comes, as it is wont to do,
The north wind falling like a wave,
To rattle window, fence and stave.

Now, the "king of the north" arrives on sleet,
To make my farm his county seat,
The mercury warns of its retreat,
As bitter cold meets body heat.

Mournful bellows, blow and puff,
Withered milkweeds crackle and scuff,
Scarecrows bend to bow and scrape,
In effort to flee and make escape.

I light my lantern to feed the stock,
Fighting through gales that whistle and mock,
I hasten hard to the henhouse door,
As chickens scatter and tumble o'er.

The icy snow pelts head and hand,
Like stinging wasps and blowing sand,
Maddening gusts spin the weather vane,
That occasionally balks to the north again.

With cattle fed and flock secure,
It's more than mortal can endure,
To follow hedges, fence and shrub,
'long clothesline, pump and washing tub.

I press my hat to warm my head,
As through the drifts of snow I tread,
To end my journey at the door,
With light and love, and Bess once more.

Words To Myself

Once inside I quickly thaw,
My stiffened gait and frozen jaw,
And rub my blurry eyes to see,
Dear Bessie pouring out my tea.

Soon my vision starts to clear,
Pretty Bess is standing near,
To dry my brow with fragrant sleeve,
And remind me that it's Christmas Eve.

Bess bids me, smiling, to keep my seat,
And taste the butternut fudge so sweet,
To show me all that she has done,
To make our holiday full and fun.

I take my session with the churn,
With golden lumps that swirl and turn,
And wash and mold them, smooth as silk,
(Then steal a sip of buttermilk!)

The yeasty smell of golden loaves,
Cinnamon, apples, spice and cloves,
A bowl of nuts and browning crust,
Pumpkin pies and sugar dust.

We settle in our favorite chair,
Like sleepy rabbits in cozy lair,
To watch the wisps of steam arise,
From simmering kettles and baking pies.

Outside, the bell upon its post,
Bangs the clapper, like a ghost,
Can the evening's darkness tame?
And bring the driving storm to shame?

58

But now is the wind a gentle breeze,
With twinkling stars on frosted seas,
Our eyes so heavy and pillows soft,
Our dreams and fantasies aloft.

But soon we'll hear the morning's thunder,
Sleigh bells shaking, children's laughter,
Mustn't linger — chores to be done!
Before the folks for breakfast, come.

But in the stable, soft and warm,
Our donkey's helpless foal is born,
A gift from God to show our worth,
To remind us of our Savior's birth.

FIRST CHRISTMAS ON THE FARM
© 1992, 2019 by Michael Leonard Jewell

To Peeps

RUSTY THE HORSE

Rusty the horse, gave me a ride,
He ran all day until I cried,
Judi laughed and Linda sighed,
Rusty, Rusty, why do you chide?

Rusty galloped down Meadowbrook Road,
He scarcely knew he carried a load,
My bottom was sore, my face was cold,
Rusty, Rusty, why so bold?

Rusty stopped at his barnyard fence,
My tears were streaming, the moment tense,
How could I have ever been so dense?
Rusty, Rusty, have you lost your sense?

Rusty "whinnied" and counted ten,
He seemed all ready to go again,
All the king's horses and all the king's men,
Rusty, Rusty, please do it again!

RUSTY THE HORSE
© 2019 by Michael Leonard Jewell

To Linda Radke and her horse Rusty—
A memory of my famous ride as a lad of eight

AUTUMN FAIR

Summer weeds have gone to seed,
Crickets chirp through rush and reed,
Flowers wave their last goodbye,
Nighthawks dart through endless sky.

Evening clouds are red and thin,
Candles glow through glass and tin,
Gases bubble in willow slough,
Grasses "wet" in the evening dew.

Pumpkins take the name of "Jack,"
Bonfires raging — sizzle and crack,
Cats chase rats and bats catch gnats,
Witches stir their simmering vats!

A yellow moon begins to rise,
Dark woods stare with silent eyes,
Black clouds make the moon's bowtie,
Riders fly their brooms on high.

Footsteps swish through unraked leaves,
Spiders lurk in sparkling weave,
Children's laughter goes unhushed,
Evening specters go unrushed.

Popcorn, candy and pale ghosts,
Apple cider and weenie roasts,
Jack o' lantern with carrot nose —
Through the night, they played . . .

Halloween is almost done,
With the rising of the sun,
November's cold and rainy skies,
Take us from making pumpkin faces,
To baking pumpkin pies.

AUTUMN FAIR
© 2019 by Michael Leonard Jewell

To my cousin Kevin Wesner

THE CAROL THAT I SEEK

The carol that I seek,
Its absence stirs my sleep,
The portent is so bleak,
Yet it's the carol that I seek.

It is almost Christmas Time,
The ivy and the vine,
Doth 'pon my brick wall creep,
Now it's the carol that I seek.

The frost upon my stone,
Greets Yuletide as is wont,
Though drifts have fallen deep,
It's the carol that I seek.

Christmastide will soon begin,
The guests shall gather anon,
The blowing snows shall sweep,
Yet it's the carol that I seek.

The repast so steaming bright,
Generates its festive light,
The folks all have their fill,
Yet it's the carol that I will.

The even' too soon has come,
The candles are guttered low,
My head desires sleep,
Yet it's the carol that I seek.

To the attic, Christmas must go,
The snowdrops soon shall peep,
For I at loss shall weep,
The carol no more to seek.

THE CAROL THAT I SEEK
© 2019 by Michael Leonard Jewell

*In honor of my mother and all the wonderful Christmases
she made for us as kids*

OLD ORCHARDS

Behind our barn on Michigan land,
A plot of ancient orchard stands,
Less tended every year—now not,
The fallen fruit is left to rot.

The farmer seems to work around,
This gnarled patch of forgotten ground,
A place of thistles and wild rice,
Where plow has failed to break and slice.

One quickly spies that every tree,
Lacks plumb and line and symmetry,
No steady rows on even land,
Just unpruned branches touch' hand to hand.

The reddish-gray and shiny bark,
All bear the wounds and subtle marks,
Of youthful sweetheart's promise say,
Now smiled upon by heads of gray.

These trunks of aging lumber stand,
With sagging arms outstretched so grand,
Not knowing if this year's their last,
To weather winter's killing blast.

The farmer's sled pulled by his mule,
Hastens there to harvest fuel,
Knowing trees that stand alone, soon,
Are only fit for hearth and home.

And of course, I know the farmer well,
(*He's married to my Grandma Nell,*)
He taught me there is nothing wrong,
When orchards deign grow old and strong.

And when in mind I visit may,
I'll disembark my father's sleigh,
To watch as Grandpa treks along,
With pail and shovel and hearty song,
To dig where frozen apples lie,
For Grandma's Sunday apple pie.

OLD ORCHARDS
© 1995, 2019 by Michael Leonard Jewell

To my Aunt Lorraine

THE END

Words To Myself

www.ingramcontent.com/pod-product-compliance
Lightning Source LLC
LaVergne TN
LVHW041207080426
835508LV00008B/836